T0085026

STEPHEN SONDHEIM
BROADWAY SOLOS

CONTENTS

THE CD IS PLAYABLE ON ANY CD PLAYER, AND IS ALSO ENHANCED SO MAC AND PC USERS CAN ADJUST THE RECORDING TO ANY TEMPO WITHOUT CHANGING THE PITCH.

ISBN 978-1-4234-7280-3

RILTING MUSIC, INC.

EXCLUSIVELY DISTRIBUTED BY

HAL•LEONARD®
CORPORATION

7777 W. BLUEMOUND RD. P.O. BOX 13819 MILWAUKEE, WI 53213

Visit Hal Leonard Online at
www.halleonard.com

ANYONE CAN WHISTLE

from ANYONE CAN WHISTLE

Words and Music by
STEPHEN SONDHEIM

TRUMPET

BEING ALIVE
from COMPANY

Music and Lyrics by
STEPHEN SONDHEIM

BROADWAY BABY

from FOLLIES

Music and Lyrics by
STEPHEN SONDHEIM

TRUMPET

5

CHILDREN WILL LISTEN
from INTO THE WOODS

7/8

TRUMPET

Words and Music by
STEPHEN SONDHEIM

COMEDY TONIGHT

from A FUNNY THING HAPPENED ON THE WAY TO THE FORUM

9/10

TRUMPET

Words and Music by
STEPHEN SONDHEIM

GOOD THING GOING

from MERRILY WE ROLL ALONG

TRUMPET

Words and Music by
STEPHEN SONDHEIM

JOHANNA
from SWEENEY TODD

Words and Music by
STEPHEN SONDHEIM

TRUMPET

LOSING MY MIND

from FOLLIES

Music and Lyrics by
STEPHEN SONDHEIM

TRUMPET

NOT A DAY GOES BY
from MERRILY WE ROLL ALONG

Words and Music by
STEPHEN SONDHEIM

TRUMPET

17/18

NOT WHILE I'M AROUND

from SWEENEY TODD

Words and Music by
STEPHEN SONDHEIM

TRUMPET

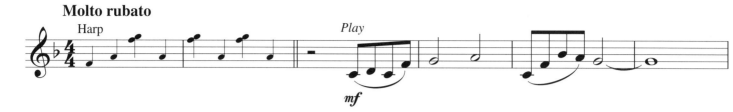

OLD FRIENDS
from MERRILY WE ROLL ALONG

Words and Music by
STEPHEN SONDHEIM

TRUMPET

21/22

PRETTY WOMEN

from SWEENEY TODD

Words and Music by
STEPHEN SONDHEIM

TRUMPET

SEND IN THE CLOWNS

from the Musical A LITTLE NIGHT MUSIC

Words and Music by
STEPHEN SONDHEIM

25/26

TRUMPET

Slowly, with feeling

SUNDAY
from SUNDAY IN THE PARK WITH GEORGE

Words and Music by
STEPHEN SONDHEIM

TRUMPET